INDULGENCE

# cupcakes

## a fine selection of sweet treats

Christabel Martin

FALL RIVER PRESS

# Contents

# Family favorites

From naughty to nice this delicious assortment will bring out the child in all of us.

# Orange poppy seed cupcakes

**MAKES 15**

**¼ cup poppy seeds, plus extra to sprinkle**
**½ cup warm milk**
**½ cup plus 1 tablespoon unsalted butter, softened**
**3 teaspoons finely grated orange zest**
**¾ cup superfine sugar**
**2 eggs**
**1½ cups self-rising flour, sifted**

**Citrus frosting**

**1 cup unsalted butter, softened**
**3 cups confectioners' sugar, sifted**
**3 teaspoons finely grated orange zest**

Preheat the oven to 350°F. Line 15 standard muffin cups with paper liners.

Combine the poppy seeds and milk in a bowl and set aside for at least 15 minutes.

Place the butter, orange zest, superfine sugar, eggs, and flour in a large bowl. Add the poppy seed mixture and beat with electric beaters on low speed until combined. Increase to a medium speed and beat for 3 minutes, or until the mixture is thick and pale.

Divide the mixture evenly among the paper liners. Bake for 15 minutes, or until a skewer comes out clean when inserted into the center of a cake. Transfer onto a wire rack to cool

To make the citrus frosting, place the butter, confectioners' sugar, and zest in a large bowl and beat with electric beaters until light and fluffy. Spread the frosting over the cakes and sprinkle with the extra poppy seeds.

# Plum crumble mini cakes

**MAKES 24**

**¾ cup unsalted butter, softened**
**¾ cup superfine sugar**
**1 teaspoon natural vanilla extract**
**3 eggs**
**1 cup self-rising flour**
**¼ cup all-purpose flour**
**½ cup canned natural plum juice**
**9 canned plums in natural juice, stones removed, thinly sliced**

**Crumble topping**
**½ cup raw sugar**
**1 cup all-purpose flour**
**heaping ⅓ cup unsalted butter, chilled and diced**

Preheat the oven to 350°F. Line 24 flat-based mini muffin cups with paper liners.

Cream the butter, sugar, and vanilla with electric beaters until light and creamy. Add the eggs one at a time, beating well after each addition. Sift the flours together and fold in alternately with the plum juice. Divide the mixture evenly among the paper liners and cover each with slices of plum.

To make the crumble topping, place the sugar, flour, and butter in a bowl. Mix together with your fingertips until it resembles coarse breadcrumbs. Sprinkle the crumble over each cake, covering the plums.

Bake for 15–18 minutes, or until golden. Transfer onto a wire rack to cool.

# Gingerbread cupcakes

**MAKES 16**

**2 cups self-rising flour**
**¾ cup all-purpose flour**
**½ teaspoon baking soda**
**3 teaspoons ground ginger**
**1 teaspoon ground cinnamon**
**1 teaspoon pumpkin pie spice**
**1 cup soft brown sugar**
**¼ cup candied ginger, chopped**
**⅔ cup maple syrup**
**heaping ⅓ cup unsalted butter, chopped**
**1 cup buttermilk**
**2 eggs, lightly beaten**

**Ginger frosting**
**2 cups confectioners' sugar, sifted**
**1 teaspoon ground ginger**
**1 tablespoon unsalted butter, softened**

Preheat the oven to 400°F. Line 16 standard muffin cups with paper liners.

Sift the flours, baking soda, ground ginger, cinnamon, and pumpkin pie spice into a large bowl. Stir in the brown sugar and candied ginger. Make a well in the center.

Put the maple syrup and butter in a small saucepan and stir over medium heat until melted. Remove from the heat and cool. Combine the syrup mixture, the buttermilk, and egg in a jug, mix together and pour into the well in the dry ingredients. Fold in gently until just combined — the batter should be lumpy.

Divide the mixture evenly among the paper liners. Bake for 20–25 minutes, or until a skewer comes out clean when inserted into the center of a cake. Transfer onto a wire rack to cool.

To make the ginger frosting, place the confectioners' sugar, ginger, and butter in a small heatproof bowl. Stir in enough warm water to form a smooth paste. Sit the bowl over a saucepan of simmering water, making sure the bowl doesn't touch the water, and stir until smooth and glossy. Remove from the heat. Spread 2 teaspoons of frosting over each cake. Sprinkle with confectioners' sugar.

# Hot cross bun cakes

**MAKES 12**

**2 cups self-rising flour**
**3 teaspoons ground cinnamon**
**½ cup unsalted butter, chopped**
**1 cup golden raisins**
**¼ cup mixed candied citrus peel**
**¾ cup superfine sugar**
**¾ cup milk**
**2 eggs, lightly beaten**

**Glaze**
**2 teaspoons powdered gelatin**
**2 tablespoons superfine sugar**

**Frosting**
**½ cup confectioners' sugar**
**2 teaspoons lemon juice**

Preheat the oven to 400°F. Grease 12 standard muffin cups.

Sift the flour and cinnamon into a large bowl, add the butter, then rub together with your fingertips until the mixture resembles fine breadcrumbs. Stir in the golden raisins, citrus peel and superfine sugar. Make a well in the center.

Whisk the milk and egg in a jug, then pour into the well. Fold in gently until just combined — the batter should be lumpy.

Divide the mixture evenly among the muffin cups. Bake for 20–25 minutes, or until the cakes come away from the side of the tin. Cool briefly, then transfer onto a wire rack.

To make the glaze, combine the gelatin, superfine sugar, and 2 tablespoons of water in a small saucepan. Stir over low heat for 1 minute, or until the sugar and gelatin are dissolved. Remove from the heat. Brush the glaze over the warm cakes a couple of times, then allow them to cool.

To make the frosting, mix the confectioners' sugar and lemon juice together until smooth. Spoon the frosting into a piping bag, and pipe a cross on each cake and allow them to set.

# Jaffa cupcakes

**MAKES 12**

**1⅓ cups self-rising flour**
**¼ cup unsweetened cocoa powder**
**1 cup superfine sugar**
**2 eggs, lightly beaten**
**⅔ cup milk**
**½ cup unsalted butter, melted**
**1 tablespoon finely grated orange zest**

**Orange buttercream**
**2 cups confectioners' sugar, sifted**
**¼ cup unsalted butter, softened**
**2 teaspoons finely grated orange zest**
**2 tablespoons orange juice**
**orange nonpareils, to decorate**

Preheat the oven to 350°F. Line 12 standard muffin cups with paper liners.

Sift the flour and cocoa into a large bowl, then stir in the sugar. Add the egg, milk, melted butter, and orange zest and beat with electric beaters for 2 minutes, or until well combined and smooth.

Divide the mixture evenly among the paper liners. Bake for 18–20 minutes, or until a skewer comes out clean when inserted into the center of a cake. Transfer onto a wire rack to cool.

To make the orange buttercream, place 1 cup of the confectioners' sugar, the butter, zest, and orange juice in a large mixing bowl. Beat with electric beaters until smooth and creamy. Gradually add the remaining confectioners' sugar and beat until the cream is thick.

Decorate each cake with buttercream and nonpareils.

# Apricot, sour cream, and coconut cupcakes

**MAKES 20**

**1¾ cups self-rising flour**
**½ cup unsweetened dried coconut**
**½ cup unsalted butter**
**1 cup superfine sugar**
**2 eggs, lightly beaten**
**1 cup apricot juice**
**½ cup sour cream**
**20 canned apricot halves in juice, drained**
**¼ cup apricot jam**

Preheat the oven to 350°F. Line 20 standard muffin cups with paper liners.

Sift the flour into a large mixing bowl, then add the coconut and make a well in the center. Melt the butter and sugar in a small saucepan over low heat, stirring until the sugar has dissolved. Remove from the heat. Whisk the combined egg and apricot juice into the sour cream. Add both the butter and the egg mixtures to the well in the dry ingredients and stir with a wooden spoon until combined.

Divide the mixture evenly among the paper liners and place an apricot half, cut side up, on the top of each cake. Bake for 18–20 minutes, or until a skewer comes out clean when inserted into the center of a cake. Transfer onto a wire rack to cool.

Heat the jam in a small saucepan until melted. Brush a little jam over each cake.

# Butterfly cupcakes

**MAKES 12**

**½ cup unsalted butter, softened**
**⅔ cup superfine sugar**
**1½ cups self-rising flour**
**½ cup milk**
**2 eggs**
**½ cup heavy cream**
**¼ cup strawberry jam**
**confectioners' sugar, to sprinkle**

Preheat the oven to 350°F. Line 12 standard muffin cups with paper liners.

Beat the butter, sugar, flour, milk, and eggs with electric beaters on low speed until combined. Increase to medium speed and beat until the mixture is smooth and pale.

Divide the mixture evenly among the paper liners and bake for 15–20 minutes, or until a skewer comes out clean when inserted into the center of a cake. Transfer onto a wire rack to cool.

Cut a shallow round from the center of each cake using the point of a sharp knife, then cut the round in half. Spoon 2 teaspoons of cream into the cavity of each cake, then top with 1 teaspoon of jam. Position the two halves of the cake round in the jam to resemble butterfly wings. Sprinkle with sifted confectioners' sugar.

# Peanut butter mini cupcakes

**MAKES 18**

**scant ⅔ cup unsalted butter, chopped**
**½ cup soft brown sugar**
**2 eggs**
**½ cup crunchy peanut butter**
**1 cup self-rising flour**
**¼ cup all-purpose flour**
**¼ cup milk**

**Hazelnut and peanut butter frosting**
**½ cup hazelnut spread, softened**
**⅓ cup crunchy peanut butter, softened**
**2 x 2¼-ounce chocolate-coated peanut bars (such as Snickers), chopped**

Preheat the oven to 350°F. Line 18 flat-based mini muffin cups with paper liners.

Beat the butter and sugar together in a bowl with electric beaters until light and creamy. Add the eggs, one at a time, beating well after each addition. Add the peanut butter and beat until combined. Fold in the sifted flours alternately with the milk until combined.

Divide the mixture evenly among the paper liners. Bake for 10–12 minutes, or until a skewer comes out clean when inserted into the center of a cake. Transfer onto a wire rack to cool completely.

To make the hazelnut and peanut butter frosting, combine the hazelnut spread and peanut butter. Spread the frosting over each cake and decorate with a piece of chocolate peanut bar.

# Jam doughnut cupcakes

**MAKES 18**

**1¼ cups self-rising flour**
**½ cup superfine sugar**
**½ cup milk**
**2 eggs**
**1 teaspoon natural vanilla extract**
**½ teaspoon dried yeast**
**½ cup strawberry jam**
**1 tablespoon unsalted butter, melted**
**2 tablespoons cinnamon sugar**

Preheat the oven to 350°F. Line 18 standard muffin cups with paper liners.

Combine the flour and sugar in a bowl, and make a well in the center. Put the milk, eggs, vanilla, and yeast in a jug and whisk to combine. Pour into the well in dry ingredients and whisk until smooth.

Divide half the mixture evenly among the paper liners. Top each with 1 teaspoon of jam, then cover with the remaining mixture. Bake for 10–12 minutes, or until a skewer comes out clean when inserted into the center of a cake. Brush a little melted butter over each cake, then dip it into the cinnamon sugar. Serve the cakes warm.

# Honey, banana, and macadamia cupcakes

**MAKES 32**

**heaping ⅓ cup unsalted butter, chopped**
**1 cup honey, plus extra to drizzle**
**2 cups self-rising flour**
**1 teaspoon pumpkin pie spice**
**1½ cups coarsely grated carrot**
**1 ripe banana, mashed**
**½ cup chopped macadamia nuts, plus extra to sprinkle**
**2 eggs, lightly beaten**

Preheat the oven to 350°F. Line 32 mini muffin cups with paper liners.

Melt the butter and honey in a small saucepan, stirring until combined. Allow to cool.

Sift the flour and pumpkin pie spice into a large bowl. Add the carrot, banana, macadamias, eggs, and honey mixture, stirring until the mixture is just combined and smooth.

Divide the mixture evenly among the paper liners, and sprinkle the tops liberally with extra chopped macadamias. Bake for 8 minutes, or until a skewer comes out clean when inserted into the center of a cake. Transfer onto a wire rack to cool.

Drizzle a little honey over the cakes before serving.

# Half-moon cupcakes

**MAKES 16**

**1 cup unsalted butter**
**1 cup superfine sugar**
**1 teaspoon natural vanilla extract**
**4 eggs**
**1½ cups self-rising flour, sifted**
**½ cup all-purpose flour, sifted**
**¾ cup milk**
**¼ cup unsweetened cocoa powder, sifted**

**Frosting**
**1½ cups confectioners' sugar, sifted**
**2 teaspoons unsalted butter**

**Chocolate topping**
**1⅓ cups chopped bittersweet chocolate**

Preheat the oven to 350°F. Line 16 standard muffin cups with paper liners.

Beat the butter, sugar, and vanilla together with electric beaters until light and creamy. Add the eggs, one at a time, beating well after each addition. Fold in the flours alternately with the milk. Divide the mixture in half and stir the cocoa through one half of the mixture until well combined. Divide the chocolate mixture evenly into half of the paper liners. Then divide the plain mixture into the other half, so that each paper liner is filled with half chocolate and half plain mixtures. Bake for 18–20 minutes, or until a skewer comes out clean when inserted into the center of a cake. Transfer onto a wire rack to cool.

To make the frosting, place the confectioners' sugar and butter in a small heatproof bowl. Stir in enough warm water to form a smooth paste. Sit the bowl over a small saucepan of simmering water and stir until smooth and glossy. Remove from the heat. Spread the frosting over the white side of each cake.

To make the chocolate topping, place the chocolate in a small bowl over a saucepan of simmering water, and stir occasionally until the chocolate has melted. Spread the chocolate over the other half of the cakes.

# Apple pecan cupcakes

**MAKES 16**

**2½ cups self-rising flour**
**1½ teaspoons ground cinnamon**
**¾ cup superfine sugar**
**2 granny smith apples, peeled, cored and coarsely grated**
**½ cup pecans, chopped**
**2 eggs, lightly beaten**
**½ cup milk**
**3 teaspoons unsalted butter, melted**
**heavy cream or yogurt, to serve (optional)**

Preheat the oven to 350°F. Line 16 standard muffin cups with paper liners.

Combine the flour, cinnamon, sugar, apple, and pecans in a bowl. Add the egg, milk, and melted butter, stirring until the mixture is just combined and smooth.

Divide the mixture evenly among the paper liners. Bake for 18–20 minutes, or until a skewer comes out clean when inserted into the center of a cake. Transfer onto a wire rack to cool.

If desired, sprinkle with confectioners' sugar and serve with heavy cream or yogurt.

# Beehive cupcakes

**MAKES 16**

**¾ cup plus 1 tablespoon unsalted butter, softened**
**1 cup soft brown sugar**
**3 eggs**
**⅓ cup honey, warmed**
**2¼ cups self-rising flour, sifted**

**Marshmallow frosting**
**3 egg whites**
**1½ cups sugar**
**2 teaspoons light corn syrup**
**pinch of cream of tartar**
**1 teaspoon natural vanilla extract**
**yellow food coloring**
**15 toothpicks**
**15 chocolate-foil wrapped bumble bees with wings**

Preheat the oven 350°F. Line 15 standard muffin cups with paper liners.

Beat the butter and sugar with electric beaters until light and creamy. Add the eggs, one at a time, beating well after each addition. Fold in the honey and flour until combined. Divide the mixture evenly among the paper liners. Bake for 18–20 minutes, or until a skewer comes out clean when inserted into the center of a cake. Transfer onto a wire rack to cool.

To make the marshmallow frosting, combine the egg whites, sugar, corn syrup, cream of tartar, and 3½ fluid ounces of water in a heatproof bowl. Sit the bowl over a saucepan of simmering water, making sure the bowl doesn't touch the water. Beat for 5 minutes with electric beaters, or until the mixture is light and fluffy. Remove from the heat. Add the vanilla and beat with electric beaters for 4–5 minutes, or until stiff peaks form. Add the coloring, drop by drop, and beat until just combined.

Spoon the frosting into a piping bag fitted with a ½-inch round nozzle, and pipe the frosting in circles around the cake to resemble a beehive. Push the pointy end of the toothpick into the base of each bee and insert it into each cake.

1½ ts. baking powder per 1c. flour

# Mini pear and walnut cupcakes

**MAKES 36**

**scant ⅔ cup unsalted butter, softened**
**¾ cup soft brown sugar**
**2 eggs**
**1¼ cups self-rising flour, sifted**
**½ cup milk**
**½ cup canned pears, well drained and chopped**
**⅓ cup chopped walnuts**

**Maple cream frosting**
**⅓ cup cream cheese, softened**
**¼ cup maple syrup**
**1½ cups confectioners' sugar, sifted**
**½ cup chopped walnuts, to decorate**

Preheat the oven to 350°F. Line 36 mini muffin cups with paper liners.

Beat the butter and sugar together with electric beaters until light and creamy. Add the eggs, one at a time, beating well after each addition. Fold in the flour alternately with the milk. Fold in the pears and the walnuts. Divide the mixture evenly among the paper liners. Bake for 12–15 minutes, or until a skewer comes out clean when inserted into the center of a cake. Transfer onto a wire rack to cool.

To make the maple cream frosting, beat the cream cheese and maple syrup with electric beaters until combined. Gradually beat in the confectioners' sugar until combined. Spread the frosting over each cake and decorate with chopped walnuts.

# Milk chocolate buttons

**MAKES 12**

**¼ cup plus 1 tablespoon unsalted butter**
**½ cup chopped milk chocolate**
**⅓ cup soft brown sugar**
**2 eggs, lightly beaten**
**½ cup self-rising flour, sifted**

**Ganache**
**½ cup chopped milk chocolate**
**2 tablespoons heavy cream**
**silver nonpareils, to decorate**

Preheat the oven to 325°F. Line 12 mini muffin cups with paper liners.

Place the butter and chocolate in a heatproof bowl and sit the bowl over a saucepan of simmering water, making sure the bowl doesn't touch the water. Stir the chocolate until melted. Remove the bowl from the heat and mix in the sugar and egg. Stir in the flour.

Transfer the mixture to a jug and pour evenly among the paper liners. Bake for 20–25 minutes, or until cooked. Leave in the tin for 10 minutes, then transfer onto a wire rack to cool completely.

To make the ganache, place the chocolate and cream in a heatproof bowl. Sit the bowl over a saucepan of simmering water, making sure the bowl doesn't touch the water. Once the chocolate has almost melted, remove the bowl from the heat and stir until the remaining chocolate has melted and the mixture is smooth. Allow to cool for about 8 minutes, or until thickened slightly.

Return the cakes to the cold tin to keep them stable while you spread 1 heaping teaspoon of ganache over each cake. Decorate with silver nonpareils.

# Banana sour cream cupcakes

**MAKES 24**

**¾ cup unsalted butter, softened**
**1 cup superfine sugar**
**3 eggs**
**2½ cups self-rising flour**
**½ teaspoon baking soda**
**¾ cup sour cream**
**2 tablespoons maple syrup**
**3 very ripe bananas, mashed**

**Honey cream frosting**
**scant ⅓ cup cream cheese, softened**
**2½ tablespoons unsalted butter, softened**
**1½ tablespoons honey**
**2 cups confectioners' sugar, sifted**

Preheat the oven to 350°F. Line 24 standard muffin cups with paper liners.

Beat the butter and sugar in a large bowl using electric beaters for 5–6 minutes, or until light and fluffy. Add the eggs, one at a time, beating well after each addition.

Sift the flour and baking soda together. Add the sour cream and maple syrup to the mashed banana and mix well. Fold the flour mixture alternately with the banana mixture in the butter mixture until well combined.

Divide the mixture evenly among the paper liners. Bake for 15 minutes, or until a skewer comes out clean when inserted into the center of a cake. Transfer onto a wire rack to cool.

To make the honey cream frosting, place the cream cheese and butter in a small bowl and beat with electric beaters until smooth. Add the honey and confectioners' sugar and beat until smooth and well combined. Decorate each cake generously with the frosting.

# Marble cupcakes

**MAKES 10**

**¾ cup unsalted butter, softened**
**¾ cup superfine sugar**
**1 teaspoon natural vanilla extract**
**3 eggs**
**1 cup self-rising flour**
**¼ cup all-purpose flour**
**½ cup milk**
**pink food coloring**
**2 tablespoons unsweetened cocoa powder, sifted**

**Marble frosting**
**2¼ cups confectioners' sugar, sifted**
**heaping ⅓ cup unsalted butter, softened**
**pink food coloring**

Preheat the oven to 350°F. Line 10 standard muffin cups with paper liners.

Beat the butter, sugar, and vanilla together with electric beaters until light and creamy. Add the eggs, one at a time, beating well after each addition. Sift the flours together and fold in alternately with the milk.

Divide the mixture into three equal portions. Add a few drops of pink food coloring to one portion and mix to combine. Add the cocoa to another portion and mix to combine. Divide the three colors evenly into each paper liner and gently swirl the mixture with a skewer. Bake for 15 minutes, or until a skewer comes out clean when inserted into the center of a cake. Transfer onto a wire rack to cool.

To make the marble frosting, mix the confectioners' sugar, butter, and enough hot water to make a spreadable frosting. Spread the frosting over each cake. Dip a skewer in pink food coloring and swirl it through the frosting to create a marbled effect.

# Pecan and orange cupcakes

**MAKES 16 or 24 mini**

**½ cup unsalted butter, softened**
**¾ cup superfine sugar**
**2 eggs**
**¾ cup ground pecans**
**3 teaspoons finely grated orange zest**
**1½ cups self-rising flour, sifted**
**½ cup milk**

**Cinnamon frosting**
**1 tablespoon unsalted butter, softened**
**¾ teaspoon ground cinnamon**
**1½ cups confectioners' sugar, sifted**

Preheat the oven to 350°F. Line 16 standard (or 24 mini) muffin cups with paper liners.

Beat the butter and sugar with electric beaters until pale and creamy. Gradually add the eggs, one at a time, beating well after each addition. Add the ground pecans and orange zest, then use a metal spoon to gently fold in the flour alternately with the milk.

Divide the mixture evenly among the paper liners. Bake for 50–60 minutes (40 minutes for minis), or until a skewer comes out clean when inserted into the center of a cake. Leave in the tin for 10 minutes, then transfer onto a wire rack to cool.

To make the cinnamon frosting, combine the butter, confectioners' sugar and cinnamon in a small bowl with 1½ tablespoons of hot water. Sit the bowl over a saucepan of simmering water, making sure the bowl doesn't touch the water, and stir until smooth and glossy. Remove from the heat. Decorate each cake with frosting.

# White chocolate chip cupcakes

**MAKES 12**

**½ cup unsalted butter, softened**
**¾ cup superfine sugar**
**2 eggs**
**1 teaspoon natural vanilla extract**
**2 cups self-rising flour, sifted**
**½ cup buttermilk**
**1¼ cups white chocolate chips**

Preheat the oven to 325°F. Line 12 standard muffin cups with paper liners.

Beat the butter and sugar in a large bowl with electric beaters until pale and creamy. Gradually add the eggs, one at a time, beating well after each addition. Add the vanilla extract and beat until combined. Fold in the flour alternately with the buttermilk, then fold in the chocolate chips.

Divide the mixture evenly among the paper liners until three-quarters full. Bake for 20 minutes, or until a skewer comes out clean when inserted into the center of a cake. Leave the cakes in the tin for 5 minutes, then transfer onto a wire rack to cool.

# Rhubarb yogurt cupcakes

**MAKES 24**

**1½ cups finely sliced fresh rhubarb, plus 24 extra pieces to garnish**
**2½ cups self-rising flour, sifted**
**1 cup superfine sugar**
**1 teaspoon natural vanilla extract**
**2 eggs, lightly beaten**
**½ cup plain yogurt**
**1 tablespoon rosewater**
**½ cup unsalted butter, melted**

Preheat the oven to 350°F. Line 24 standard muffin cups with paper liners.

Combine the rhubarb, flour, and sugar in a bowl. Add the vanilla, egg, yogurt, rosewater, and the melted butter, stirring with a wooden spoon until the mixture is just combined.

Divide the mixture evenly among the paper liners, then top with a piece of rhubarb. Bake for 15 minutes, or until a skewer comes out clean when inserted into the center of a cake. Transfer onto a wire rack to cool.

# Apple and raisin cupcakes

**MAKES 12**

**1½ cups self-rising flour**
**scant ⅔ cup unsalted butter, chopped**
**¾ cup soft brown sugar**
**1 cup raisins, plus extra to garnish**
**½ cup apple purée**
**3 eggs, lightly beaten**

**Yogurt topping**
**1 cup plain yogurt**
**1 tablespoon soft brown sugar**

Preheat the oven to 350°F. Line 12 standard muffin cups with paper liners.

Sift the flour into a large bowl and make a well in the center. Melt the butter and sugar in a small saucepan over a low heat, stirring until the sugar has dissolved. Remove from the heat. Combine the raisins and apple purée with the butter mixture. Pour into the well in the flour, along with the egg. Stir with a wooden spoon until combined.

Divide the mixture evenly among the paper liners. Bake for 15 minutes, or until a skewer comes out clean when inserted into the center of a cake. Transfer onto a wire rack to cool completely.

To make the yogurt topping, combine the yogurt and sugar. Spread 1 tablespoon of topping over each cake.

# Sweet afternoons

These elegant offerings call for an aromatic hot tea to be sipped slowly from your finest china cup.

# Pistachio and cardamom cupcakes

**MAKES 24**

**1 cup unsalted pistachio pieces**
**½ teaspoon ground cardamom, plus extra to sprinkle**
**scant ⅔ cup unsalted butter, chopped**
**1½ cups self-rising flour**
**¾ cup superfine sugar**
**3 eggs**
**½ cup plain yogurt**

**Lime syrup**
**½ cup superfine sugar**
**zest of 1 lime, white pith removed**

**Honey yogurt topping**
**1 cup plain yogurt**
**1 tablespoon honey**

Preheat the oven to 350°F. Line 24 standard muffin cups with paper liners.

Place the pistachios and cardamom in a food processor and pulse until just chopped. Add the butter, flour, and superfine sugar and pulse for 20 seconds, or until crumbly. Add the eggs and yogurt and pulse until just combined.

Divide the mixture evenly among the paper liners. Bake for 15 minutes, or until a skewer comes out clean when inserted into the center of a cake. Transfer onto a wire rack to cool.

To make the lime syrup, place the superfine sugar and 3½ fluid ounces of water in a small saucepan and stir over low heat until the sugar has dissolved. Bring to a boil, then add the zest and cook for 5 minutes. Strain. Brush the syrup over the cakes while they're still warm, then allow to cool.

To make the honey yogurt topping, place the yogurt and honey in a small bowl and stir until well combined. Decorate each cake with the honey yogurt and a sprinkle of ground cardamom.

# Fruit tart cupcakes

**MAKES 12**

**¾ cup unsalted butter, softened**
**¾ cup superfine sugar**
**1 teaspoon natural vanilla extract**
**3 eggs**
**1 cup self-rising flour**
**¼ cup all-purpose flour**
**½ cup milk**
**½ cup thick ready-made custard**
**1 kiwi fruit, peeled**
**1 cup strawberries**
**1 freestone peach, peeled**
**red grapes (about 4 to 6)**
**½ cup apricot jam**

Preheat the oven to 350°F. Line 12 standard muffin cups with paper liners.

Beat the butter, sugar, and vanilla together with electric beaters until light and creamy. Add the eggs, one at a time, beating well after each addition. Sift the flours together and fold in alternately with the milk.

Divide the mixture evenly among the paper liners. Bake for 15 minutes, or until a skewer comes out clean when inserted into the center of a cake. Transfer onto a wire rack to cool.

Cut the center out of each cake, leaving a ½-inch border. Fill each cavity with 2 teaspoons of custard. Cut the fruit and arrange over the custard. Heat the jam until runny. Lightly brush the jam over the top of each cake. Refrigerate until ready to serve.

# Chocolate and almond cupcakes

**MAKES 36**

**⅔ cup chopped bittersweet chocolate**
**½ cup ground almonds**
**¾ cup self-rising flour**
**4 eggs, separated**
**½ cup superfine sugar**
**2 tablespoons warm milk**
**chocolate flakes, to decorate**
**unsweetened cocoa powder, to sprinkle**

**Chocolate ganache**
**⅔ cup chopped bittersweet chocolate**
**heaping ⅓ cup unsalted butter**

Preheat the oven to 350°F. Line 36 mini muffin cups with paper liners.

Place the chocolate in a food processor and process until finely ground. Add the ground almonds and flour and process until just combined.

Beat the egg yolks and sugar with electric beaters for 2–3 minutes, or until thick and pale. Stir in the chocolate mixture, then the milk. Beat the egg whites in a clean bowl until soft peaks form. Gently fold the whites into the mixture with a metal spoon until just combined. Divide the mixture evenly among the paper liners. Bake for 10–12 minutes, or until a skewer comes out clean when inserted into the center of a cake. Transfer onto a wire rack to cool.

To make the chocolate ganache, place the chocolate and butter in a small heatproof bowl over a saucepan of simmering water, making sure the bowl doesn't touch the water. Stir until smooth and combined. Refrigerate for 20 minutes, stirring occasionally until thickened.

Cut the center out of the cakes. Fill each cavity with 1 teaspoon of chocolate ganache, then decorate with chocolate flakes and cocoa.

# Mandarin and chamomile cupcakes

**MAKES 20**

**¾ cup milk**
**¼ cup chamomile tea flowers, plus extra to decorate**
**scant ⅔ cup unsalted butter, chopped**
**1 cup superfine sugar**
**3 eggs**
**2 teaspoons finely grated mandarin zest**
**6 mandarins (about 10½ ounces), peeled, seeds removed**
**½ cup fine semolina**
**1¼ cups self-rising flour**

**Mandarin glaze**
**1¼ cups confectioners' sugar, sifted**
**1 teaspoon finely grated mandarin zest**
**2–3 tablespoons strained, fresh mandarin juice**
**chamomile tea flowers, to garnish**

Preheat the oven to 350°F. Line 20 mini muffin cups with paper liners.

Place the milk and chamomile tea flowers into a saucepan and bring just to a boil. Stand for 5 minutes to infuse. Strain.

Place the butter, sugar, eggs, mandarin zest, and mandarin in a food processor and process until almost smooth. Add the milk mixture, semolina, and flour and process until smooth. Pour the mixture evenly among the paper liners. Bake for 8–10 minutes, or until a skewer comes out clean when inserted into the center of a cake. Transfer onto a wire rack to cool.

To make the mandarin glaze, place the confectioners' sugar, zest, and enough juice to make a paste in a heatproof bowl. Sit the bowl over a saucepan of simmering water, making sure the base of the bowl doesn't touch the water, and stir until runny. Remove from the heat but keep the bowl over the water. Spread the glaze over each cake and decorate with a chamomile flower.

# Individual blueberry cheesecakes

**MAKES 6**

**Cheese mixture**
**½ cup superfine sugar**
**⅓ cup cream cheese**

**Blueberry sauce**
**1⅔ cups blueberries**
**1 tablespoon crème de cassis**

**1⅓ cups all-purpose flour**
**1 tablespoon baking powder**
**1 tablespoon unsalted butter, melted**
**1 teaspoon finely grated orange zest**
**1 egg**
**½ cup milk**
**18 blueberries, plus extra for filling**
**confectioners' sugar, to sprinkle**

Preheat the oven to 350°F. Lightly grease 6 standard muffin cups with butter or oil.

To make the cheese mixture, put half the sugar in a bowl with the cream cheese and mix together well.

To make the blueberry sauce, put the blueberries in a blender or food processor with the liqueur and remaining sugar, and blend until smooth. Strain the mixture through a fine sieve to remove any blueberry seeds. Set the cheese mixture and sauce aside.

Sift the flour and baking powder together in a large bowl and stir in the butter, orange zest, and ½ teaspoon of salt. In a separate bowl, beat the egg and milk together, then add to the dry ingredients and mix well until combined.

Divide half the mixture evenly among the cups. Add three of the extra blueberries and 1 teaspoon of cheese mixture in each cup, then top with the remaining batter mixture. Bake for 15 minutes, or until cooked and golden. Transfer onto a wire rack to cool slightly. To serve, put each cheesecake on a plate, drizzle with blueberry sauce and sprinkle with confectioners' sugar.

# Prune and ricotta cupcakes

**MAKES 18**

**⅓ cup pitted prunes, chopped**
**1 tablespoon Marsala**
**1 cup ricotta cheese**
**½ cup superfine sugar**
**2 eggs**
**¼ cup whipping cream**
**¼ cup cornstarch, sifted**
**2 tablespoons self-rising flour, sifted**
**¼ cup grated bittersweet chocolate**
**confectioners' sugar, to sprinkle**

Preheat the oven to 350°F. Line 18 mini muffin cups with paper casses.

Combine the prunes and Marsala in a small saucepan. Bring to a boil, then reduce the heat and simmer for 30 seconds, or until the Marsala is absorbed. Allow to cool.

Beat the ricotta and sugar with electric beaters for 2 minutes, or until light and creamy. Gradually add the eggs, one at a time, beating well after each addition. Add the cream and beat for 2 minutes. Using a metal spoon, fold in the sifted cornstarch and flour, the prune mixture and the chocolate.

Divide the mixture evenly among the paper liners. Bake for 15–18 minutes, or until firm and lightly golden. Transfer onto a wire rack to cool. Sprinkle with confectioners' sugar just before serving.

Mode de Paris

# Orange and lemon syrup cupcakes

**MAKES 36**

**½ cup unsalted butter, chilled and chopped**
**1 cup superfine sugar**
**2 teaspoons finely grated lemon zest**
**2 teaspoons finely grated orange zest**
**3 eggs**
**½ cup milk**
**1½ cups self-rising flour, sifted**

**Lemon syrup**
**1 cup superfine sugar**
**zest of 1 lemon, thinly sliced**
**zest of 1 orange, thinly sliced**

Preheat the oven to 350°F. Line 36 mini muffin cups with paper liners.

Place the butter, sugar, and lemon and orange zests in a saucepan and stir over low heat until the sugar has dissolved. Transfer to a large bowl. Add the eggs, milk and flour and beat with electric beaters until just combined.

Divide the mixture evenly among the paper liners. Bake for 15 minutes, or until a skewer comes out clean when inserted into the center of a cake. Transfer onto a wire rack to cool.

To make the lemon syrup, place 7 fluid ounces of water and the sugar in a saucepan over low heat, stirring until the sugar has dissolved. Add the lemon and orange zests, bring to a boil and simmer for 10 minutes, stirring occasionally, or until lightly golden and syrupy.

Strain the syrup, reserving the zest. Decorate each cake with some strips of zest and pour over a little of the syrup.

# Fluffy coconut cupcakes

**MAKES 36**

**2 cups self-rising flour, sifted**
**½ cup unsweetened dried coconut**
**1 cup superfine sugar**
**1 cup buttermilk**
**2 eggs, lightly beaten**
**1 teaspoon natural coconut extract**
**½ cup unsalted butter, melted**

**Coconut frosting**
**2¼ cups confectioners' sugar**
**1½ cups unsweetened dried coconut**
**¼ cup plus 1 tablespoon unsalted butter, softened**
**½ teaspoon natural coconut extract**
**2 tablespoons hot water**
**unsweetened dried coconut, lightly toasted, to sprinkle**

Preheat the oven to 350°F. Line 36 mini muffin cups with paper liners.

Combine the flour, coconut, and sugar in a bowl and make a well in the center. Pour in the combined buttermilk, eggs, coconut extract, and butter into the well and mix until combined.

Divide the mixture evenly among the paper liners. Bake for 12 minutes, or until a skewer comes out clean when inserted into the center of a cake. Transfer onto a wire rack to cool.

To make the coconut frosting, combine the confectioners' sugar and coconut in a bowl. Add the butter, coconut extract, and enough hot water to make a spreadable frosting. Decorate each cake with a thick covering of frosting and sprinkle with toasted coconut.

# Hazelnut cream sponge cakes

**MAKES 16**

**4 eggs, separated**
**½ cup superfine sugar**
**½ cup self-rising flour**
**⅔ cup ground hazelnuts**
**1 tablespoon unsalted butter**

**Hazelnut frosting**
**½ cup chocolate hazelnut spread**
**heaping ½ cup unsalted butter, softened**
**½ cup confectioners' sugar, sifted**

Preheat the oven to 350°F. Grease a shallow 8-inch square cake tin and line the base with parchment paper.

Beat the egg whites in a clean bowl with electric beaters until soft peaks form. Gradually add the sugar, beating until thick and glossy. Beat the egg yolks into the mixture, one at a time.

Sift the flour over the mixture, add the ground hazelnuts and fold in with a metal spoon. Melt the butter with 2 tablespoons of boiling water in a small bowl, then fold into the sponge mixture. Pour the mixture into the tin and bake for 25 minutes, or until a skewer comes out clean when inserted into the center of the cake. Leave in the tin for 5 minutes before turning out onto a wire rack to cool. Cut the sponge in half horizontally through the center.

To make the hazelnut frosting, beat the chocolate hazelnut spread and butter with electric beaters until very creamy. Beat in the confectioners' sugar, then gradually add 3 teaspoons of boiling water and beat until smooth. Spread the frosting over the base of the sponge, then replace the top layer. Refrigerate until the filling is firm, then cut into squares and place inside paper liners.

# Streusel cupcakes

**MAKES 24**

**Custard**
**3 egg yolks**
**2 tablespoons superfine sugar**
**2 tablespoons instant custard powder**
**1 cup milk**
**1 teaspoon natural vanilla extract**

**Topping**
**½ cup all-purpose flour**
**⅔ cup finely chopped walnuts**
**½ cup soft brown sugar**
**scant ⅓ cup unsalted butter, melted**
**1 teaspoon ground cinnamon**

**¾ cup unsalted butter, softened**
**¾ cup superfine sugar**
**1 teaspoon natural vanilla extract**
**3 eggs**
**1 cup self-rising flour**
**¼ cup all-purpose flour**
**1 teaspoon pumpkin pie spice**
**½ cup golden raisins**
**½ cup milk**

Preheat the oven to 350°F. Line 24 standard muffin cups with paper liners.

To make the custard, place the egg yolks, sugar, and custard powder in a bowl and whisk until pale. Heat the milk in a small saucepan until almost boiling. Remove from the heat, then gradually whisk into the egg mixture. Return the combined mixture to the cleaned saucepan and stir constantly over low heat until the mixture boils and thickens. Refrigerate until cold.

To make the topping, mix all the ingredients together in a bowl, until the mixture resembles coarse breadcrumbs.

Beat the butter, sugar, and vanilla together with electric beaters until light and creamy. Add the eggs, one at a time, beating well after each addition. Sift the flours and pumpkin pie spice together and fold in alternately with the golden raisins and milk. Swirl the custard through the mixture, but do not overmix. Divide the mixture evenly among the paper liners. Sprinkle the topping over the cakes. Bake for 14–15 minutes, or until a skewer comes out clean when inserted into the center of a cake. Transfer onto a wire rack to cool.

# Passionfruit cupcakes

**MAKES 15**

**¾ cup unsalted butter, softened**
**¾ cup superfine sugar**
**1 teaspoon natural vanilla extract**
**3 eggs**
**½ cup cream cheese, softened**
**1 tablespoon fresh passionfruit pulp (about 1 passionfruit)**
**1 cup self-rising flour**
**¼ cup all-purpose flour**
**¼ cup milk**

**Passionfruit frosting**
**1¼ cups whipping cream**
**1½ tablespoons confectioners' sugar, sifted**
**2 tablespoons fresh passionfruit pulp (about 2 passionfruit)**

Preheat the oven to 350°F. Line 15 standard muffin cups with paper liners.

Beat the butter, sugar, and vanilla together with electric beaters until light and creamy. Add the eggs, one at a time, beating well after each addition. Add the cream cheese and passionfruit and beat until smooth. Sift the flours together and fold in alternately with the milk.

Divide the mixture evenly among the paper liners. Bake for 15 minutes, or until a skewer comes out clean when inserted into the center of a cake. Transfer onto a wire rack to cool.

To make the passionfruit frosting, beat the cream and confectioners' sugar together until soft peaks form. Cut the center out of each cake leaving a ½-inch border. Spoon the cream into a piping bag fitted with a ½-inch star nozzle. Decorate each cake with piped cream and top with the passionfruit.

# Baklava cupcakes

**MAKES 36**

**Filling**
**½ cup walnuts, chopped**
**⅓ cup blanched almonds, chopped**
**½ cup raw sugar**
**2 teaspoons ground cinnamon**
**2½ tablespoons unsalted butter, melted**

**¾ cup unsalted butter, softened**
**¾ cup soft brown sugar**
**3 eggs**
**1 cup self-rising flour**
**¼ cup all-purpose flour**
**½ cup buttermilk**
**¼ cup honey, warmed**

Preheat the oven to 350°F. Line 36 mini muffin cups with paper liners.

Combine the filling ingredients in a bowl and set aside.

Beat the butter and sugar in a bowl with electric beaters until light and creamy. Add the eggs, one at a time, beating well after each addition. Fold in the sifted flours alternately with the milk, and stir until smooth and combined.

Divide half the mixture evenly among the paper liners. Sprinkle half the filling over the mixture, then spoon the remaining mixture over the top. Sprinkle over the remaining filling. Bake for 10–12 minutes, or until a skewer comes out clean when inserted into the center of a cake. Brush warm honey over the cakes while they are still hot.

# Plum and almond cupcakes

**MAKES 18**

**1½ cups self-rising flour**
**1½ teaspoons ground cinnamon**
**heaping ⅓ cup unsalted butter, melted**
**1 cup soft brown sugar**
**3 eggs, lightly beaten**
**⅓ cup blanched almonds, finely chopped**
**1 pound 13-ounce can pitted plums in natural juice, drained and chopped**
**dried rose petals, to decorate**

**White chocolate cream frosting**
**1⅓ cups chopped white chocolate**
**½ cup whipping cream**
**heaping ¾ cup cream cheese, softened**
**⅓ cup confectioners' sugar, sifted**
**pink food coloring**

Preheat the oven to 325°F. Line 18 standard muffin cups with paper liners.

Sift the flour and cinnamon together in a bowl. Add the butter, sugar, eggs, almonds, and plums and mix with electric beaters until combined.

Divide the mixture evenly among the paper liners. Bake for 15 minutes, or until a skewer comes out clean when inserted into the center of a cake. Transfer onto a wire rack to cool.

To make the white chocolate cream frosting, combine the chocolate and cream in a small saucepan and stir over low heat until the chocolate has melted. Place the chocolate mixture, cream cheese, and confectioners' sugar in a bowl and beat with electric beaters until smooth. Add a few drops of red food coloring and blend evenly. Cover the bowl and refrigerate for 2 minutes, or until slightly firm. Beat the mixture again for a few seconds until smooth.

Spread the frosting over each cake and decorate with the dried rose petals.

# Mango cakes with lime syrup

**MAKES 8**

**1 pound 14-ounce can mango slices in syrup, drained**
**¾ cup unsalted butter, softened**
**1 cup superfine sugar**
**4 eggs**
**1 cup self-rising flour**
**⅓ cup ground almonds**
**⅓ cup coconut milk**

**Lime syrup**
**⅓ cup lime juice**
**½ cup superfine sugar**

Preheat the oven to 400°F. Grease 8 large muffin cups, then line with the mango slices.

Beat the butter and sugar in a bowl with electric beaters until light and creamy. Gradually add the eggs, one at a time, beating well after each addition. Fold in the flour, then add the almonds and coconut milk.

Divide the mixture evenly among the cups. Bake for 25 minutes, or until a skewer comes out clean when inserted into the center of a cake.

To make the lime syrup, place the lime juice, sugar, and ½ cup of water in a small saucepan and stir over low heat until the sugar dissolves. Increase the heat and simmer for 10 minutes.

Pierce holes in each cake with a skewer. Drizzle the syrup over the top and leave for 5 minutes to soak up the liquid. Turn out onto plates and serve.

# Madeira cupcakes

**MAKES 12**

**¾ cup unsalted butter, softened**
**¾ cup superfine sugar**
**3 eggs**
**1⅓ cups all-purpose flour**
**2 teaspoons baking powder**
**1 teaspoon finely grated orange zest**
**1 tablespoon orange juice**

**Orange frosting**
**2 cups confectioners' sugar, sifted, plus extra to spinkle**
**½ cup unsalted butter, softened**
**1 tablespoon orange juice**

Preheat the oven to 350°. Line 12 standard muffin cups with paper liners.

Beat the butter and sugar in a bowl with electric beaters until pale and light. Add the eggs, one at a time, beating well after each addition. Sift the flour and baking powder together. Fold the flour, orange zest, and juice into the butter mixture until combined.

Divide the mixture evenly among the paper liners. Bake for 12–15 minutes, or until a skewer comes out clean when inserted into the center of a cake. Transfer onto a wire rack to cool completely.

To make the orange frosting, place the confectioners' sugar, butter, and juice in a large bowl and beat with electric beaters until smooth and well combined. Decorate each cake with frosting and sprinkle with confectioners' sugar.

# Chestnut cupcakes

**MAKES 36**

**½ cup unsalted butter, softened**
**1 cup superfine sugar**
**1 teaspoon natural vanilla extract**
**½ cup unsweetened chestnut purée**
**3 eggs**
**⅓ cup milk**
**1¼ cups self-rising flour, sifted**
**1 teaspoon baking powder**
**36 flower frosting decorations**

**Chocolate glaze**
**1⅔ cups chopped bittersweet chocolate**
**¾ cup whipping cream**

Preheat the oven to 350°F. Line 36 mini muffin cups with paper liners.

Beat the butter, sugar, and vanilla with electric beaters until light and creamy. Add the chestnut purée and beat for 1 minute, or until just combined. Add the eggs, one at a time, beating well after each addition. Fold in the milk, flour, and baking powder, and stir with a wooden spoon until the ingredients are just combined.

Divide the mixture evenly among the paper liners. Bake for 15 minutes, or until a skewer comes out clean when inserted into the center of a cake. Transfer onto a wire rack to cool completely.

To make the chocolate glaze, combine the chocolate and cream in a small saucepan. Stir over low heat until the chocolate has melted and the mixture is smooth. Remove from the heat and cool slightly.

Dip the top of each cake into the glaze to coat and decorate each with an frosting flower.

# Saffron spice cupcakes

**MAKES 24**

**¾ cup orange juice**
**3 teaspoons finely grated orange zest**
**¼ teaspoon saffron threads**
**2 eggs**
**1 cup confectioners' sugar**
**1 teaspoon natural vanilla extract**
**1½ cups self-rising flour**
**1½ cups ground almonds**
**heaping ⅓ cup unsalted butter, melted**

**Saffron threads**
**½ teaspoon saffron threads**
**2 tablespoons orange juice**

**Mascarpone cream**
**1 cup plus 2 tablespoons mascarpone cheese**
**½ cup confectioners' sugar, sifted**
**¼ teaspoon ground cardamom**

Preheat the oven to 350°F. Line 24 standard muffin cups with paper liners.

Combine the orange juice, zest, and saffron in a small saucepan and bring to a boil. Reduce the heat and simmer for 1 minute. Leave to cool.

Beat the eggs, confectioners' sugar, and vanilla with electric beaters until light and creamy. Fold in the sifted flour, almonds, orange juice mixture, and butter with a metal spoon until combined. Divide the mixture evenly among the paper liners. Bake for 18–20 minutes, or until a skewer comes out clean when inserted into the center of a cake. Transfer onto a wire rack to cool.

To make the saffron threads, place the saffron and orange juice in a small saucepan and bring to a simmer for 1 minute. Strain and discard the orange juice. Set the saffron threads aside.

To make the mascarpone cream, place the mascarpone, sugar, and cardamom in a small bowl and mix to combine (be careful not to overmix or it may curdle). Decorate each cake with piped cream and top with the saffron threads.

# Coconut, ginger, and lime cupcakes

**MAKES 36**

**scant ⅔ cup unsalted butter, softened**
**¾ cup superfine sugar**
**2 teaspoons finely grated lime zest**
**2 eggs**
**¼ cup finely chopped candied ginger**
**1¾ cups self-rising flour**
**½ cup unsweetened dried coconut**
**¾ cup milk**

**Lime frosting**
**1 cup confectioners' sugar, sifted**
**2 teaspoons unsalted butter, softened**
**1 teaspoon finely grated lime zest**
**2 tablespoons lime juice**

Preheat the oven to 350°F. Line 36 mini muffin cups with paper liners.

Beat the butter, sugar, and lime zest with electric beaters until light and creamy. Add the eggs, one at a time, beating well after each addition. Add the ginger. Stir in the sifted flour and the coconut alternately with the milk.

Divide the mixture evenly among the paper liners. Bake for 15 minutes, or until a skewer comes out clean when inserted into the center of a cake. Transfer onto a wire rack to cool.

To make the lime frosting, combine all of the ingredients, adding enough lime juice to make a smooth, runny frosting. Decorate each cake with frosting.

# Hawaiian macadamia cupcakes

**MAKES 18**

**1½ cups self-rising flour**
**½ teaspoon ground cinnamon**
**¾ cup superfine sugar**
**½ cup unsweetened dried coconut**
**3 eggs, lightly beaten**
**7¾-ounce can crushed pineapple in syrup, drained**
**¾ cup vegetable oil**
**⅓ cup macadamia nuts, chopped, plus extra to decorate**

**Lemon cream**
**⅓ cup cream cheese, softened**
**2½ tablespoons unsalted butter, softened**
**1½ tablespoons lemon juice**
**2¼ cups confectioners' sugar, sifted**

Preheat the oven to 350°F. Line 18 standard muffin cups with paper liners.

Sift the flour and cinnamon into a large bowl, then add the sugar and coconut and stir to combine. Add the egg, pineapple, and oil and mix well. Stir in the macadamia nuts.

Divide the mixture evenly among the paper liners. Bake for 18–20 minutes, or until a skewer comes out clean when inserted into the center of a cake. Transfer onto a wire rack to cool.

To make the lemon cream, beat the cream cheese and butter in a large bowl with electric beaters until smooth. Add the lemon juice and confectioners' sugar, and beat until well combined.

Decorate each cake with the lemon cream and a sprinkling of macadamia nuts.

# Sour cherry cupcakes

**MAKES 18**

**½ cup unsalted butter, softened**
**¾ cup superfine sugar**
**2 eggs**
**1½ cups self-rising flour**
**½ cup milk**
**1 cup pitted morello cherries, well drained, halved**

Preheat the oven to 350°F. Line 18 standard muffin cups with paper liners.

Beat the butter and sugar with electric beaters until pale but not creamy. Add the eggs, one at a time, beating well after each addition. Fold in the sifted flour alternately with the milk. Gently fold in the cherries.

Divide the mixture evenly among the paper liners. Bake for 18–20 minutes, or until a skewer comes out clean when inserted into the center of a cake. Transfer onto a wire rack to cool. Sprinkle with confectioners' sugar before serving. These cakes are best eaten on the day they're made.

# Sweet basil and olive oil cupcakes

**MAKES 18**

**3 eggs**
**1 cup superfine sugar**
**3 teaspoons finely grated orange zest**
**3 teaspoons finely grated lemon zest**
**¾ cup olive oil**
**2½ cups self-rising flour**
**⅓ cup milk**
**⅓ cup orange juice**

**Creamy basil frosting**
**3 cups confectioners' sugar, sifted**
**⅓ cup unsalted butter, softened**
**¼ cup milk**
**1 teaspoon natural vanilla extract**
**2 tablespoons finely chopped basil, plus small basil leaves to decorate**

Preheat the oven to 350°F. Line 18 standard muffin cups with paper liners.

Whisk the eggs and sugar in a large bowl until well combined. Add the orange and lemon zests, then stir in the olive oil. Stir in the sifted flour alternately with the milk and orange juice. Stir the mixture gently for 30 seconds with a wooden spoon.

Divide the mixture evenly among the paper liners. Bake for 15 minutes, or until a skewer comes out clean when inserted into the center of a cake. Transfer onto a wire rack to cool.

To make the creamy basil frosting, place half the confectioners' sugar, butter, milk, vanilla, and chopped basil in a large mixing bowl and beat with electric beaters until smooth and creamy. Gradually add the remaining confectioners' sugar until the frosting is thick. Decorate each cake with the frosting and a small basil leaf.

# Pink coconut cupcakes

**MAKES 12**

**¾ cup unsalted butter, softened**
**¾ cup superfine sugar**
**1 teaspoon natural vanilla extract**
**2 eggs**
**1 cup self-rising flour**
**¼ cup all-purpose flour**
**½ cup milk**
**3 tablespoons strawberry jam**

**Pink frosting**
**1 cup confectioners' sugar, sifted**
**2 teaspoons unsalted butter, softened**
**pink food coloring**
**⅓ cup strawberry jam, sieved**
**⅓ cup unsweetened dried coconut, to sprinkle**

Preheat the oven to 350°F. Line 12 standard muffin cups with paper liners.

Beat the butter, sugar, and vanilla together with electric beaters until light and creamy. Add the eggs, one at a time, beating well after each addition. Sift the flours together and fold in alternately with the milk. Gently stir through the jam, being careful not to overmix it. You want it to swirl through.

Divide the mixture evenly among the paper liners. Bake for 15 minutes, or until a skewer comes out clean when inserted into the center of a cake. Transfer onto a wire rack to cool.

To make the pink frosting, place the confectioners' sugar and butter in a bowl and add enough hot water to make a spreadable consistency. Add just a few drops of food coloring to make a pale pink frosting. Spread the frosting over the cakes. Place the sieved jam in a piping bag fitted with a ½-inch plain nozzle. Pipe the jam down the center of each cake, then sprinkle with the coconut.

# Middle Eastern orange curd cupcakes

**MAKES 24**

**¾ cup self-rising flour**
**½ cup fine semolina**
**½ cup ground almonds**
**1 teaspoon ground cardamom**
**¾ cup superfine sugar**
**½ cup unsalted butter, melted**
**2 eggs, lightly beaten**
**⅓ cup milk**

**Orange curd**
**2 egg yolks**
**1 egg**
**¼ cup superfine sugar**
**2 teaspoons finely grated blood orange zest**
**¼ cup blood orange juice**
**¼ cup plus 1 tablespoon unsalted butter**
**pistachio pieces, to decorate**

Preheat the oven to 350°F. Line 24 mini muffin cups with paper liners.

Place the sifted flour and semolina into a bowl with the almonds, cardamom, and sugar. Make a well in the center. Whisk the butter, egg, and milk in a jug to combine. Pour into the well and mix until combined.

Divide the mixture evenly among the paper liners. Bake for 10–12 minutes, or until a skewer comes out clean when inserted into the center of a cake. Transfer onto a wire rack to cool.

To make the orange curd, whisk the yolks, egg, sugar, and zest together in a saucepan until combined. Add the juice and butter and whisk over a low heat for 2–3 minutes, or until the curd thickens. Transfer to a bowl and refrigerate until cold. Spread the curd over each cake and decorate with pistachios.

# Dressed to impress

When only the best will do, a decadent selection for the cupcake sophisticate.

# Semolina berry cupcakes

**MAKES 24**

**1 cup fine semolina**
**½ cup self-rising flour, sifted**
**1 teaspoon baking powder, sifted**
**¾ cup superfine sugar**
**¾ cup unsalted butter, melted**
**1 teaspoon natural vanilla extract**
**1 cup plain yogurt**
**1¼ cups fresh raspberries (or frozen, thaw before use)**

**Sugared raspberries**
**2 cups fresh raspberries**
**1 egg white, lightly beaten**
**⅓ cup superfine sugar**

**Frosting**
**½ cup unsalted butter, softened**
**1½ cups confectioners' sugar, sifted**
**2 teaspoons milk**

Preheat the oven to 350°F. Line 24 standard muffin cups with paper liners.

Place the semolina, flour, baking powder, and sugar in a bowl. Combine the melted butter, vanilla, and yogurt, then add to the dry ingredients. Stir the mixture until smooth and just combined. Stir through the raspberries.

Divide the mixture evenly among the paper liners. Bake for 15 minutes, or until a skewer comes out clean when inserted into the center of a cake. Transfer onto a wire rack to cool.

To make the sugared raspberries, lightly brush each berry with egg white, then dip in the sugar to coat. Place the raspberries on a cookie sheet lined with parchment paper and set aside for 1 hour to dry.

To make the frosting, beat the butter, sugar, and milk in a medium bowl using electric beaters until smooth and combined. Decorate each cake with the frosting and top with a sugared raspberry.

# Rich dark chocolate cupcakes

**MAKES 18**

**scant ⅔ cup unsalted butter, chopped**
**1¼ cups bittersweet chocolate chips**
**1½ cups self-rising flour**
**¼ cup unsweetened cocoa powder**
**1¼ cups superfine sugar**
**2 eggs, lightly beaten**
**chocolate curls, to decorate**

**Chocolate topping**
**1⅔ cups chopped bittersweet chocolate**
**2 tablespoons unsalted butter**

Preheat the oven to 325°F. Line 18 standard muffin cups with paper liners.

Place the butter and chocolate chips in a small heatproof bowl. Sit the bowl over a saucepan of simmering water, making sure the bowl doesn't touch the water. Stir the chocolate constantly until it is melted.

Sift the flour and cocoa into a large bowl. Combine the melted butter and chocolate mixture, sugar, and egg, then add ¾ cup of water and mix well. Add to the dry ingredients and stir until well combined. Divide the mixture evenly among the paper liners. Bake for 20–25 minutes, or until a skewer comes out clean when inserted into the center of a cake. Transfer onto a wire rack to cool.

To make the chocolate topping, place the chocolate and butter in a small heatproof bowl and sit it over a saucepan of simmering water, making sure the base of the bowl doesn't touch the water. Stir the chocolate constantly until it melts. Decorate each cake with the topping and chocolate curls.

# Strawberry swirl cupcakes

**MAKES 12**

**¾ cup unsalted butter, softened**
**¾ cup superfine sugar**
**3 eggs**
**1 cup self-rising flour**
**¼ cup all-purpose flour**
**½ cup milk**
**¼ teaspoon pink food coloring**

**Liqueur strawberries**
**2 teaspoons confectioners' sugar, sifted**
**1 tablespoon strawberry liqueur**
**6 strawberries, hulled and halved**
**small scoops strawberry ice cream**

Preheat the oven to 350°F. Line 12 standard muffin cups with paper liners.

Beat the butter and sugar together with electric beaters until light and creamy. Add the eggs, one at a time, beating well after each addition. Sift the flours together and fold in alternately with the milk. Add the food coloring and lightly swirl through the mixture to create a marbled effect.

Divide the mixture evenly among the paper liners. Bake for 15 minutes, or until a skewer comes out clean when inserted into the center of a cake. Transfer onto a wire rack to cool.

Combine the confectioners' sugar and liqueur and stir to dissolve the sugar. Add the strawberries and stir to combine. Set aside to macerate for 5 minutes.

Cut out the center of each cake leaving a ½-inch border. Top each cake with a scoop of ice cream and decorate with a strawberry liqueur.

# Sticky date cupcakes

**MAKES 6**

**1½ cups pitted dates, chopped**
**1 teaspoon baking soda**
**¼ cup unsalted butter, chopped**
**1½ cups self-rising flour**
**⅔ cup soft brown sugar**
**2 eggs, lightly beaten**
**ice cream, to serve**

**Sauce**
**2 tablespoons maple syrup**
**¾ cup whipping cream**
**⅓ cup unsalted butter, chopped**
**¾ cup soft brown sugar**

Preheat the oven to 350°F. Grease 6 large muffin cups.

Place the dates and 1 cup of water in a saucepan and bring to a boil. Remove from the heat and stir in the baking soda. Add the butter and stir until melted.

Sift the flour into a large bowl, then add the sugar and stir. Make a well in the center. Add the date mixture and egg and stir until just combined. Divide the mixture evenly among the cups. Bake for 20 minutes, or until a skewer comes out clean when inserted into the center of a cake. Allow to cool, then transfer onto serving plates.

To make the sauce, place the maple syrup, cream, butter, and sugar in a small saucepan and stir over low heat for 3–4 minutes, or until the sugar has dissolved. Bring to a boil, then reduce the heat and simmer, stirring occasionally, for 2 minutes. Pierce the cakes a few times with a skewer, then drizzle with the sauce. Serve with a scooop of ice cream.

DISTRIBUTED BY REX C. NORRIS PTY. LTD.
BUTTONS BY Rex
WILL LAUNDER and DRY CLEAN

# Decadent double chocolate mousse cupcakes

**MAKES 24**

**¾ cup all-purpose flour**
**¼ cup self-rising flour**
**½ cup unsalted butter, chopped**
**1 cup superfine sugar**
**⅔ cup chopped white chocolate**
**1 egg**
**1 teaspoon natural vanilla extract**
**½ cup milk**

**Chocolate mousse**
**1 egg yolk**
**2 tablespoons superfine sugar**
**2 cups whipping cream**
**1¼ cups bittersweet chocolate chips, melted**

Preheat the oven to 325°F. Line 24 standard muffin cups with paper liners.

Sift the flours together in a bowl and make a well. Place the butter, sugar, and chocolate in a saucepan and stir over low heat until the sugar has dissolved. Remove from the heat and cool slightly.

Whisk the egg, vanilla, and milk to combine, then pour into the well in the flour, together with the chocolate mixture, and whisk to combine. Divide the mixture evenly among the paper liners, until half-full. Bake for 15 minutes, or until a skewer comes out clean when inserted into the center of a cake. Transfer onto a wire rack to cool completely.

To make the chocolate mousse, place the egg yolk and sugar in a small bowl and whisk over a small saucepan of simmering water until thick and creamy.

Beat the cream in a bowl with electric beaters until soft peaks form. Add the melted chocolate and the egg mixture and continue to beat for 1–2 minutes, or until thickened. Decorate the cakes with the mousse, then place them on a tray and refrigerate for 1 hour, or until set. Sprinkle with cocoa before serving.

# Flourless orange and almond dessert cupcakes

**MAKES 24**

**2 oranges**
**1½ cups ground almonds**
**1 cup superfine sugar**
**1 teaspoon baking powder**
**1 teaspoon natural vanilla extract**
**1 teaspoon Cointreau or orange-flavored liqueur**
**6 eggs, lightly beaten**
**⅓ cup flaked almonds, lightly toasted, to decorate**

**Orange cream**
**2 cups sour cream**
**1 cup confectioners' sugar, sifted**
**2 teaspoons finely grated orange zest**

Place the whole oranges in a saucepan, cover with water and place a small plate on top to keep the oranges submerged. Gradually bring to a boil, then reduce the heat and simmer for 40 minutes, or until very soft.

Preheat the oven to 350°F. Line 24 standard muffin cups with paper liners.

Cut the oranges into quarters and leave to cool. Remove any pips, then blend in a food processor until very smooth. Add the ground almonds, sugar, baking powder, vanilla, and liqueur and pulse until just combined. Add the egg and process again until just combined.

Divide the mixture evenly among the paper liners. Bake for 15–18 minutes, or until firm. Leave to cool in the tin.

To make the orange cream, whisk the sour cream, confectioners' sugar, and orange zest together until thickened. Decorate each cake with the frosting and flaked almonds.

# Turkish delight cupcakes

**MAKES 36**

**¾ cup unsalted butter, softened**
**1½ cups superfine sugar**
**3 eggs**
**1½ cups self-rising flour**
**½ cup all-purpose flour**
**1 cup unsweetened cocoa powder**
**½ cup milk**
**3 x 2⅔-ounce bars chocolate-coated Turkish delight, cut into ½ inch pieces**

**Rosewater frosting**

**2 cups confectioners' sugar, sifted**
**1 tablespoon rosewater**
**2 drops pink food coloring**
**Turkish delight (not chocolate coated), to decorate**

Preheat the oven to 350°F. Line 36 mini muffin cups with paper liners.

Beat the butter and sugar together with electric beaters until light and creamy. Add the eggs, one at a time, beating well after each addition. Sift the flours and cocoa together and fold in alternately with the milk. Stir through the Turkish delight. Divide the mixture evenly among the paper liners. Bake for 18–20 minutes, or until a skewer comes out clean when inserted into the center of a cake. Transfer onto a wire rack to cool.

To make the rosewater frosting, place the confectioners' sugar in a large bowl. Add the rosewater and 1½ tablespoons of boiling water, and stir until smooth (add a little more water if necessary to make a pouring consistency). Add the food coloring (add more food coloring if desired) and stir until well combined. Spread the frosting over each cake, then decorate with pieces of Turkish delight.

# Champagne jelly cupcakes

**MAKES 36**

**scant ⅔ cup unsalted butter, chopped**
**½ cup superfine sugar**
**1 teaspoon natural vanilla extract**
**2 eggs**
**1½ cups self-rising flour, sifted**
**⅓ cup ground almonds**
**½ cup milk**
**1 cup fresh or frozen blackberries**

**Champagne jelly**
**1 bottle sparkling wine**
**2 tablespoons powdered gelatin**
**¾ cup sugar**
**36 fresh blackberries**

Preheat the oven to 350°F. Line 36 standard muffin cups with paper liners.

Beat the butter, sugar, and vanilla with electric beaters until light and creamy. Add the eggs, one at a time, beating well after each addition. Fold in the flour and almonds alternately with the milk and blackberries until combined. Divide the mixture evenly among the paper liners until half-full. Bake for 10–12 minutes, or until a skewer comes out clean when inserted into the center of a cake. Leave in the tins to cool.

To make the champagne jelly, place 2 cups of the sparkling wine in a bowl and allow the bubbles to subside. Sprinkle over the gelatin. Place the remaining sparkling wine in a saucepan with the sugar and stir over low heat until the sugar dissolves. Remove from the heat, add the gelatin mixture and stir until the gelatin has dissolved. Refrigerate for 45 minutes, or until the jelly starts to set.

Decorate each cake with jelly and top with a blackberry. Refrigerate the cakes in the tins until set.

# Lemon meringue cupcakes

**MAKES 12**

**1¾ cup self-rising flour**
**¾ cup superfine sugar, plus extra to sprinkle**
**1 egg**
**1 egg yolk**
**⅔ cup milk**
**½ teaspoon natural vanilla extract**
**⅓ cup unsalted butter, melted and cooled**
**⅔ cup ready-made lemon curd**
**2 egg whites**

Preheat the oven to 400°F. Lightly grease 12 standard muffin cups.

Sift the flour into a large bowl and stir in ¼ cup of the superfine sugar. Make a well in the center.

Place the egg and egg yolk in a bowl and add a pinch of salt. Beat the eggs together, then stir in the milk, vanilla, and butter. Pour the egg mixture into the well in the dry ingredients. Fold in gently until just combined — the mixture should be lumpy.

Divide the mixture evenly among the cups. Bake for 15 minutes — the cakes will only rise a little way up the cups. (Leave the oven on the same temperature.)

Cool the cakes in the tin for 10 minutes, then loosen with a knife but leave in the tin. Hollow out the center of each cake with a melon baller, being careful not to pierce through the base of the cake.

Stir the lemon curd well, then spoon into a piping bag fitted with a ½-inch plain nozzle. Carefully pipe the curd into the cavity of each cake.

Whisk the egg whites in a clean dry bowl until soft peaks form. Add a quarter of the remaining sugar at a time, beating well after each addition, until stiff and glossy peaks form.

Place 1 heaping tablespoon of the meringue mixture on top of each cake and form peaks with the back of a spoon. Sprinkle a little of the extra superfine sugar over the meringue.

Return the cakes to the oven for 5 minutes, or until the meringue is lightly golden and crisp and the cakes come away slightly from the side of the tin. Cool in the tin for 10 minutes, then carefully transfer onto a wire rack. The meringue topping might come off the cakes when they first come out of the oven, so handle the cakes carefully. The meringues will adhere to the cakes as they cool.

Serve warm or at room temperature. The cakes are best eaten on the day they are made so that the meringue stays crispy.

VARIATION: You can also use other flavors of citrus curds, such as lime or orange, to fill the cakes.

# Pretty in pink butter cupcakes

**MAKES 16**

**¾ cup unsalted butter, softened**
**¾ cup superfine sugar**
**3 eggs**
**1 teaspoon natural vanilla extract**
**1¼ cups self-rising flour**
**¼ cup all-purpose flour**
**½ cup milk**
**silver nonpareils, to decorate**

**Buttercream**
**1 cup unsalted butter, softened**
**2 cups confectioners' sugar, sifted**
**⅓ cup whipping cream**
**pink food coloring**

Preheat the oven to 350°F. Line 16 muffin cups with paper liners.

Beat the butter and sugar with electric beaters until light and creamy. Add the eggs, one at a time, beating well after each addition. Add the vanilla and beat until combined. Sift the flours together and fold in alternately with the milk. Stir until the ingredients are just combined and the mixture is almost smooth.

Divide the mixture evenly among the paper liners. Bake for 15–18 minutes, or until a skewer comes out clean when inserted into the center of a cake. Transfer onto a wire rack to cool.

To make the buttercream, beat the butter and confectioners' sugar with electric beaters until smooth and combined. Add the cream and beat for 30 seconds, or until fluffy. Add a few drops of pink food coloring and stir until well combined and the desired pink is achieved. Decorate each cake with the buttercream and silver nonpareils.

# Croquembouche cupcakes

**MAKES 16**

**Puffs**
**1¼ cups all-purpose flour**
**scant ⅓ cup unsalted butter**
**5 eggs**

**Filling**
**1 cup milk**
**2 egg yolks**
**2 tablespoons superfine sugar**
**2 tablespoons all-purpose flour**
**1½ tablespoons Grand Marnier**
**¾ cup whipping cream, whipped**

**Cupcakes**
**¾ cup unsalted butter, softened**
**¾ cup superfine sugar**
**1 teaspoon natural vanilla extract**
**3 eggs**
**1 cup self-rising flour**
**½ cup all-purpose flour**
**½ cup milk**

**Toffee**
**1½ cups superfine sugar**

Preheat the oven to 425°F. Line baking sheets with parchment paper.

To make the puffs, sift the flour three times onto a piece of parchment paper. Place the butter in a saucepan with 1¼ cups of water and stir until the mixture comes to a boil. Remove from the heat. Add the flour and beat until combined. Return to the heat and beat with a wooden spoon until the mixture forms a ball and leaves the side of the pan. Transfer to a large bowl and cool slightly. Add the eggs, one at a time, beating well after each addition until the mixture is thick and glossy.

Pipe heaping teaspoons of the mixture onto the baking sheets, leaving room for spreading (you need 48 puffs). Sprinkle the mixture with a little water and bake for 10 minutes, or until browned. Make a small hole in the base of each puff. Reduce the heat to 350°F and bake for a further 5 minutes to dry out.

To make the filling, place the milk in a saucepan and bring just to a boil. Remove from the heat and cool slightly. Beat the egg yolks, sugar, and flour in a bowl until thick and pale. Gradually whisk in the milk. Return to a clean saucepan and stir over medium heat until the mixture boils and thickens. Remove from the heat and stir through the Grand Marnier. Cover the surface with plastic wrap and refrigerate until cold. Fold in the whipped cream.

To make the cupcakes, line 16 standard muffin cups with paper liners. Beat the butter, sugar, and vanilla together with electric beaters until light and creamy. Add the eggs, one at a time, beating well after each addition. Sift the flours together and fold in alternately with the milk.

Divide the mixture evenly among the paper liners. Bake for 15 minutes, or until a skewer comes out clean when inserted into the center of a cake. Transfer onto a wire rack to cool.

Cut the tops of the cakes to make them flat. Spoon the filling into a piping bag fitted with a ½-inch round nozzle. Pipe the filling into the holes in the puffs. Arrange the puffs in a pyramid shape on the top of each cake, using the filling to stick them together.

To make the toffee, place the sugar and ⅔ cup of water into a small saucepan and stir over low heat until the sugar has dissolved. Bring to a boil, then reduce the heat slightly and cook for 10 minutes without stirring, or until golden. Remove from the heat and drizzle the toffee over the puffs.

# White chocolate and macadamia cupcakes

**MAKES 12**

**¾ cup unsalted butter, softened**
**¾ cup superfine sugar**
**1 teaspoon natural vanilla extract**
**3 eggs**
**1 cup self-rising flour**
**¼ cup all-purpose flour**
**½ cup milk**
**⅔ cup chopped white chocolate**
**½ cup macadamia nuts, chopped**
**ready-made frosting decorations, such as tiny butterflies**

**Royal frosting**
**2 cups confectioners' sugar, sifted**
**2 egg whites**

Preheat the oven to 350°F. Line 12 standard muffin cups with paper liners.

Beat the butter, sugar, and vanilla together with electric beaters until light and creamy. Add the eggs, one at a time, beating well after each addition. Sift the flours together and fold in alternately with the milk, chocolate, and macadamia.

Divide the mixture evenly among the paper liners. Bake for 15 minutes, or until a skewer comes out clean when inserted into the center of a cake. Transfer onto a wire rack to cool.

To make the royal frosting, beat the confectioners' sugar and egg whites together for 5 minutes until white and glossy. Decorate each cake with the frosting and little frosting decorations.

# Chocolate cherry cupcakes

**MAKES 12**

**4 x 2-ounce chocolate-coated cherry bars, chopped**
**1 cup unsalted butter, chopped**
**1 cup soft brown sugar**
**1 teaspoon natural vanilla extract**
**1¼ cups self-rising flour**
**2 tablespoons unsweetened cocoa powder**
**½ cup unsweetened dried coconut**
**3 eggs**
**12 fresh cherries, to decorate**

**Chocolate frosting**

**2 cups confectioners' sugar, sifted**
**½ cup unsweetened cocoa powder**
**1 tablespoon unsalted butter, softened**

Preheat the oven to 325°F. Line 12 standard muffin cups with paper liners.

Place the cherry bars, butter, sugar, and vanilla in a heatproof bowl. Sit the bowl over a saucepan of simmering water, making sure the bowl doesn't touch the water, and stir until the chocolate has melted.

Sift the flour and cocoa powder into a large bowl, then add the coconut. Add the chocolate mixture and the eggs and mix until combined.

Divide the mixture evenly among the paper liners. Bake for 18–20 minutes, or until a skewer comes out clean when inserted into the center of a cake. Transfer onto a wire rack to cool.

To make the chocolate frosting, place the confectioners' sugar and cocoa into a large bowl. Add the butter and enough boiling water to make a smooth and spreadable consistency. Spread the frosting over each cake and decorate with a cherry.

# Rum and raisin cupcakes

**MAKES 24**

**1 cup raisins**
**¼ cup rum**
**¾ cup soft brown sugar, 1 tablespoon extra**
**¾ cup unsalted butter, softened**
**2 eggs, lightly beaten**
**2 cups self-rising flour, sifted**
**½ cup buttermilk**
**24 raisins, to decorate**

**Rum buttercream**
**2 teaspoons instant coffee granules**
**1 cup unsalted butter, softened**
**3 cups confectioners' sugar, sifted**
**¼ cup rum**

Preheat the oven to 350°F. Line 24 mini muffin cups with paper liners.

Combine the raisins, rum, and extra 1 tablespoon of brown sugar in a small saucepan. Bring to a boil, then reduce the heat and simmer for 30 seconds, or until the rum has absorbed. Set aside to cool.

Beat the butter and brown sugar with electric beaters until pale and creamy. Add the egg — the mixture may look curdled but once you add the flour, it will bring it back together. Use a metal spoon to fold the sifted flour and buttermilk in two batches. Fold in the raisin and rum mixture.

Divide the mixture evenly among the paper liners. Bake for 15 minutes, or until a skewer comes out clean when inserted into the center of a cake. Transfer onto a wire rack to cool.

To make the rum buttercream, dissolve the coffee in 1 tablespoon of boiling water. Beat the butter and confectioners' sugar with electric beaters until light and creamy. Add half the rum and the coffee mixture and beat for 2 minutes, or until smooth and fluffy. Soak the raisins in the remaining rum. Decorate each cake with the frosting and top with a raisin.

# Chocolate cupcakes with ice cream

**MAKES 10**

- **¾ cup unsalted butter**
- **scant 1½ cups superfine sugar**
- **2½ teaspoons natural vanilla extract**
- **3 eggs**
- **⅔ cup self-rising flour, sifted**
- **1¾ cups all-purpose flour, sifted**
- **1½ teaspoons baking soda, sifted**
- **¾ cup unsweetened cocoa powder**
- **1 cup buttermilk**
- **small scoops vanilla ice cream**

Preheat the oven to 350°F. Lightly grease 10 standard muffin cups with melted butter or oil.

Beat the butter and sugar with electric beaters until light and creamy. Beat in the vanilla. Add the eggs, one at a time, beating well after each addition.

Fold in the combined flours, baking soda and cocoa powder with a metal spoon, alternately with the buttermilk. Stir until just smooth.

Divide the mixture evenly among the cups. Bake for 25 minutes, or until a skewer comes out clean when inserted into the center of a cake. Leave the cakes to cool in the tins for 5 minutes, then transfer onto a wire rack to cool completely.

Cut out the center of each cake, leaving a ½-inch border around the top. Keep the tops of the cakes to one side. Fill the center of each cake with a small scoop of ice cream, then decorate with the cake top.

# Frangipani cupcakes

**MAKES 16**

**¾ cup unsalted butter, softened**
**¾ cup superfine sugar**
**1 teaspoon natural vanilla extract**
**3 eggs**
**1 cup self-rising flour**
**½ cup all-purpose flour**
**½ cup milk**
**1 cup pink and white mini marshmallows**
**8 white marshmallows, quartered**
**8 pink marshmallows, quartered**
**yellow decorating gel**

**Frosting**
**3 cups confectioners' sugar, sifted**
**2 egg whites**
**pink food coloring**

Preheat the oven to 350°F. Line 16 standard muffin cups with large paper liners.

Beat the butter, sugar, and vanilla together with electric beaters until light and creamy. Add the eggs, one at a time, beating well after each addition. Sift the flours together and fold in alternately with the milk. Stir through the mini marshmallows until combined.

Divide the mixture evenly among the paper liners. Bake for 15 minutes, or until a skewer comes out clean when inserted into the center of a cake. Transfer onto a wire rack to cool.

To make the frosting, beat the confectioners' sugar and egg whites together for 5 minutes until white and fluffy. Divide the frosting evenly into two separate bowls. Color one with food coloring to make a pale pink.

Decorate half the cakes with pink frosting and arrange white marshmallow quarters to resemble a flower on each cake. Repeat with the white frosting and pink marshmallows for the remaining cakes. Squeeze a dollop of the yellow gel in the center of all the marshmallow petals.

# Mint slice cakes

**MAKES 12**

**¾ cup unsalted butter, softened**
**¾ cup superfine sugar**
**1 teaspoon natural vanilla extract**
**3 eggs**
**1 cup self-rising flour**
**¼ cup all-purpose flour**
**½ cup unsweetened cocoa powder**
**½ cup milk**

**Peppermint cream**
**¼ cup whiping cream**
**2 teaspoons vegetable oil**
**1 tablespoon liquid glucose**
**2 cups confectioners' sugar, sifted**
**peppermint extract**

**Ganache**
**1 cup chopped bittersweet chocolate**
**⅓ cup whipping cream**

To make the peppermint cream, combine all of the ingredients except the peppermint extract in a saucepan. Stir over low heat until the mixture is smooth and creamy. Add a few drops of peppermint and mix well. Refrigerate until ready to use.

Preheat the oven to 350°F. Line 12 standard muffin cups with paper liners.

Beat the butter, sugar, and vanilla together with electric beaters until light and creamy. Add the eggs, one at a time, beating well after each addition. Sift the flours and cocoa together and fold in alternately with the milk. Divide the mixture evenly among the paper liners. Bake for 15 minutes, or until a skewer comes out clean when inserted into the center of a cake. Transfer onto a wire rack to cool.

Remove the cakes from the paper liners and cut in half horizontally. Spread the bottom layers with peppermint cream, then replace the top layers.

To make the ganache, combine the chocolate and cream in a small saucepan. Stir over low heat until the chocolate has melted. Remove from the heat and cool. Decorate the cakes with the ganache. Keep the cakes refrigerated until ready to serve.

# Caramel toffee cupcakes

**MAKES 12**

**¾ cup unsalted butter, softened**
**¾ cup superfine sugar**
**3 eggs**
**1 cup ready-made thick, caramel filling**
**1 cup self-rising flour**
**¼ cup all-purpose flour**
**2 tablespoons milk**

**Caramel frosting**
**1½ cups confectioners' sugar, sifted**
**1 tablespoon unsalted butter, softened**
**½ cup ready-made thick, caramel filling**

**Toffee**
**½ cup superfine sugar**
**1 tablespoon lemon juice**

Preheat the oven to 350°F. Line 12 standard muffin cups with paper liners.

Beat the butter and sugar together with electric beaters until light and creamy. Add the eggs, one at a time, beating well after each addition. Add the caramel and beat until combined. Sift the flours together and fold in alternately with the milk. Divide the mixture evenly among the paper liners. Bake for 15 minutes, or until a skewer comes out clean when inserted into the center of a cake. Transfer onto a wire rack to cool.

To make the caramel frosting, beat all of the ingredients with electric beaters until smooth. Refrigerate until ready to use.

To make the toffee, line a sheet with parchment paper. Place the sugar and lemon juice in a small heavy-based saucepan over low heat, shaking the pan occasionally, until the sugar melts and becomes a light caramel. Pour the toffee onto the sheet and spread out very thinly. Set aside to cool and harden.

Spread the caramel frosting over the cakes. Peel the paper away from the toffee and break into shards. Decorate each cake with some toffee shards.

# Mini Christmas pudding cakes

**MAKES 12**

**4 cups golden raisins**
**3 cups raisins, chopped**
**1⅔ cups currants**
**1 cup quartered candied cherries**
**1 cup brandy or rum, plus 1 tablespoon to glaze**
**1 cup unsalted butter**
**1 cup soft dark brown sugar**
**2 tablespoons apricot jam**
**2 tablespoons light treacle**
**1 tablespoon finely grated lemon or orange zest**
**4 eggs**
**2¾ cups all-purpose flour**
**1 teaspoon each of ground ginger, pumpkin pie spice and cinnamon**
**silver nonpareils, to decorate**

**Royal frosting**
**1 egg white**
**2 cups confectioners' sugar, sifted**
**2–3 teaspoons lemon juice**

Put the fruit in a bowl with the brandy and leave to soak overnight.

Preheat the oven to 300°F. Lightly grease 12 mini muffin cups and line the bases with a circle of parchment paper.

Beat the butter and sugar to just combine. Beat in the jam, treacle, and zest. Add the eggs, one at a time, beating after each addition.

Stir the soaked fruit and the combined sifted flour and spices alternately into the butter mixture. Divide the mixture evenly among the cups, right to the top, smoothing the top. Bake for 40 minutes, or until a skewer comes out clean when inserted into the center of a cake. Cool in the tins, then turn out cakes onto a wire rack so that the base becomes the top.

To make the royal frosting, lightly beat the egg white with a wooden spoon. Gradually add the confectioners' sugar, beating to a smooth paste. Slowly add enough of the lemon juice until slightly runny. Decorate each cake with the frosting, using a palette knife to smooth, and letting some drizzle down the sides. Decorate with silver nonpareils.

# Cream brûlée cupcakes

**MAKES 12**

**¾ cup unsalted butter, softened**
**¾ cup superfine sugar**
**1 teaspoon natural vanilla extract**
**3 eggs**
**1 cup self-rising flour**
**¼ cup all-purpose flour**
**½ cup milk**
**¼ cup soft brown sugar**

**Cream filling**
**1½ cups milk**
**3 egg yolks**
**¼ cup superfine sugar**
**2 tablespoons all-purpose flour**

Preheat the oven to 350°F. Line 12 standard muffin cups with paper liners.

Beat the butter, sugar, and vanilla together with electric beaters until light and creamy. Add the eggs, one at a time, beating well after each addition. Sift the flours together and fold in alternately with the milk. Divide the mixture evenly among the paper liners. Bake for 15 minutes, or until a skewer comes out clean when inserted into the center of a cake. Transfer onto a wire rack to cool.

To make the cream filling, place the milk in a saucepan and bring just to a boil. Remove from the heat. Beat the egg yolks, sugar, and flour until thick and pale. Gradually whisk in the milk. Return to the saucepan and stir over medium heat until the mixture boils and thickens. Remove from the heat.

Cut out the center of the cakes, leaving a ½-inch border. Fill in the cavity of the cakes with the cream filling. Refrigerate until cold. Sprinkle 1 teaspoon of the brown sugar over each cake and place under a hot broiler for 3 minutes, or until caramelized.

# Green tea cupcakes

**MAKES 24**

**½ cup milk**
**3 teaspoons matcha (fine green tea powder)**
**¾ cup unsalted butter, softened**
**¾ cup superfine sugar**
**1 teaspoon natural vanilla extract**
**3 eggs**
**1 cup self-rising flour**
**¼ cup all-purpose flour**
**¼ cup canned sweet adzuki beans, to decorate**

**Cream**
**1 cup whipping cream**
**2 tablespoons confectioners' sugar, sifted**

Preheat the oven to 350°F. Line 24 standard muffin cups with paper liners.

Place the milk in a saucepan and bring just to a boil. Remove from the heat and whisk in the matcha. Allow to cool.

Beat the butter, sugar, and vanilla together with electric beaters until light and creamy. Add the eggs, one at a time, beating well after each addition. Sift the flours together and fold in alternately with the milk mixture. Divide the mixture evenly among the paper liners. Bake for 10–12 minutes, or until a skewer comes out clean when inserted into the center of a cake. Transfer onto a wire rack to cool.

Beat the cream and confectioners' sugar until stiff peaks form. Decorate each cake with cream and sweet adzuki beans.

# Truffle cupcakes

**MAKES 18**

**¾ cup plus 1 tablespoon unsalted butter**
**1⅓ cups chopped bittersweet chocolate**
**½ cup coffee liqueur**
**¾ cup self-rising flour**
**¾ cup all-purpose flour**
**¾ cup unsweetened cocoa powder, plus extra to sprinkle**
**½ teaspoon baking soda**
**1½ cups superfine sugar**
**3 eggs**
**1½ tablespoons oil**
**⅓ cup milk**
**bittersweet, milk and white chocolate truffles, to decorate**

**Milk chocolate ganache**
**1 cup milk chocolate chips**
**½ cup unsalted butter, chopped**
**¼ cup whipping cream**

Preheat the oven to 325°F. Line 18 standard muffin cups with paper liners.

Place the butter, chocolate, and liqueur in a saucepan and stir over low heat until melted. Remove from the heat.

Sift the flours, cocoa, and baking soda into a large bowl. Stir in the sugar and make a well in the center. Add the combined eggs, oil, and milk and gradually pour into the well, along with the chocolate mixture, mixing until combined. Divide the mixture evenly among the paper liners until three-quarters full. Bake for 25 minutes, or until a skewer comes out clean when inserted into the center of a cake. Transfer onto a wire rack to cool.

To make the milk chocolate ganache, place all of the ingredients in a saucepan and stir over low heat until melted. Transfer to a bowl and allow to cool completely. Beat with electric beaters until thick and creamy. Decorate each cake with the ganache and a piece of truffle. Sprinkle with cocoa to serve.

# Christening cupcakes

**MAKES 16**

**¾ cup unsalted butter, softened**
**¾ cup superfine sugar**
**1 teaspoon natural vanilla extract**
**3 eggs**
**1 cup self-rising flour**
**¼ cup all-purpose flour**
**½ cup milk**

**Frosting decoration**
**1 pound 2 ounces ready-made white frosting**
**1 egg white, lightly beaten**
**pink or blue food coloring**

Preheat the oven to 350°F. Line 16 standard muffin cups with paper liners.

Beat the butter, sugar, and vanilla together with electric beaters until light and creamy. Add the eggs, one at a time, beating well after each addition. Sift the flours together and fold in alternately with the milk. Divide the mixture evenly among the paper liners. Bake for 15 minutes, or until a skewer comes out clean when inserted into the center of a cake. Transfer onto a wire rack to cool.

To decorate the cakes, roll out 13 ounces of the white frosting onto a surface dusted with confectioners' sugar, to ¼ inch thick. Using a 2¾-inch round cutter, cut out 16 rounds. Lightly brush the egg white over each cake and place a round of frosting on top.

Add 1 drop of the pink or blue food coloring to the remaining frosting and knead until the coloring is well blended. Weigh 32 x 1-ounce portions of frosting. Roll out each portion into a short sausage shape. Make a bootie by bending the sausage in half. Hollow out the top of the bootie with the rounded end of a small wooden spoon, then thin the edges to make a frill. Lightly brush egg white under each pair of booties and place on top of the cake. Repeat with the remaining cupcakes and frosting.

# Index

This 2009 edition published by Fall River Press,
by arrangement with Murdoch Books Pty Limited.



Chief Executive: Juliet Rogers
Publishing Director: Kay Scarlett

Publisher: Jane Lawson
Editor: Sandra Davies
Design concept: Reuben Crossman
Design layout: Melanie Ngapo
Photographer: Brett Stevens
Stylist: Lynsey Fryers

Fall River Press
122 Fifth Avenue
New York, NY 10011

ISBN: 978-1-4351-1399-2

Printed in China by 1010 Printing International Limited

1 3 5 7 9 10 8 6 4 2

IMPORTANT: Those who might be at risk from the effects of salmonella poisoning (the elderly, pregnant women, young children, and those suffering from immune deficiency diseases) should consult their doctor with any concerns about eating raw eggs.

OVEN GUIDE: You may find cooking times vary depending on the oven you are using. For fan-forced ovens, as a general rule, set the oven temperature to 25°F lower than indicated in the recipe.